"Offering words of wisdom and joy throughout, Naomi Summers' new book *The Pond That Ripples* is replete with inspiration, delight, and reflection on what makes a good life. What is faith but 'seeing it all happen before it does'? What is beauty but what 'rises from the ashes'? Summers presents to the reader a life lived with courage, integrity, and acceptance of imperfections—yet always lit by love, both human and divine. In fact, the love of God undergirds Summers' outlook and radiates in some of her most beautiful poems, like the evocation of God's majesty in 'Guiding Light' and the well-crafted and heartwarming artistry of 'Companion.' What matters to Summers are the small, intimate gestures of a look, a smile, a touch, proving that life need not be like a grand adventure in a movie so much as the day-to-day habits of a life lived for God and for others. Pick up this collection and be encouraged to pursue your destiny with honor. Be it savored on a fire-lit evening or enjoyed in a cozy house on a rainy afternoon, *The Pond That Ripples* will stay on your mind."

—Susan Weiner, author of *Before the Foundation of the World* and *All This and More: Poems of Faith for Children and Adults*

"Within the pages of this poetry book, I found a profound resonance that spoke to both my body and soul. Through the lens of love, joy, loss, hope, faith, overcoming, and the unique experiences of being a Black woman, the author beautifully captures the complexities of the human experience. Each verse is a testament to resilience, healing, and the power of storytelling to bridge divides and cultivate understanding. A must-read for anyone seeking solace, inspiration, and a deeper connection to the heart of humanity."

—Lataya E. Hawkins, PhD, LCSW-S

The POND That RIPPLES

The POND That RIPPLES

Tammi Summers

BELLE ISLE BOOKS
www.belleislebooks.com

Copyright © 2024 by Tammi Summers

No part of this book may be reproduced in any form or by any electronic or mechanical means, or the facilitation thereof, including information storage and retrieval systems, without permission in writing from the publisher, except in the case of brief quotations published in articles and reviews. Any educational institution wishing to photocopy part or all of the work for classroom use, or individual researchers who would like to obtain permission to reprint the work for educational purposes, should contact the publisher.

ISBN: 978-1-962416-46-7
Library of Congress Control Number: 2024910923

Printed in the United States of America

Published by
Belle Isle Books (an imprint of Brandylane Publishers, Inc.)
5 S. 1st Street
Richmond, Virginia 23219

BELLE ISLE BOOKS
www.belleislebooks.com

belleislebooks.com | brandylanepublishers.com

A special thank you to my army officer friend, Magda Rodriguez-Feliz, who believed in the strength of my creative writing and encouraged me to consolidate and publish my poems so many years ago—you set my dreams of being published to flight, and I am eternally grateful.

I dedicate this book to every person I've served with over my many years in the United States Armed Forces, domestically and abroad; to numerous dear friends and comrades; and to my loving family, including my mother and father, my twin sister, my brothers, and their children.

The Pond that Ripples is dedicated to every person that dreams of living a life that is meaningful, impactful, courageous, and authentic.

I pray this book inspires you, soothes you, and reminds you that you are not alone in your hopes, your dreams, or even your struggles—and that every day presents opportunities to become the person you've always dreamed you'd be.

Table of Contents

Introduction

Poetry

Justice's Pursuit 7

The Story of Us 9

Cold Stone 10

Discover Me 11

No Hiding 12

Collision 14

Live Pursuit 15

An Imperfect Woman's Prayer 16

She Dares 17

Destiny's Azimuth 18

Continuum 19

Poetry 20

Captivate Me 21

Guiding Light 22

The Father's Cocoon 23

Companion 24

Reflections

Mirror, Mirror 27

Shine Bright 28

Human 29

Flesh and Blood 30

Ears to Hear 31

Love Freely 32

The Hard Parts 33

Survive 34

Synchronize 35

Thoughts 36

Perspective 37

Precepts 38

Her 39

Scars 40

Regeneration 41

Love's Light 42

Beyond the Sun 43

Quotes

About the Author 69

Introduction

It is said that words hold the power to shape our understanding of the world, to pierce the depths of our emotions, and to provoke profound contemplation. In *The Pond that Ripples* by Tammi Summers, we embark on a poetic journey where words transcend mere communication, becoming the conduits of spirit and life. With an unparalleled artistry, Tammi delicately wields language, inviting readers to explore the recesses of their emotions, unearthing sentiments long forgotten.

Tammi Summers fearlessly confronts the complexities of our existence, delving into challenging subjects such as race, equality, spirituality, and the inherent unfairness that life can impose. Through her prose, she navigates the turbulent waters of human experience, guiding readers through a range of emotions that resonate with authenticity. Faced with discomfort and vulnerability, Tammi returns with passages akin to healing salves, offering solace for the wounded soul.

The Pond that Ripples is not a mere collection of words; it is an intimate exploration of the human condition. Tammi peels back the layers of pain, laying bare her heart and soul upon the pages. As the reader immerses themself in the narrative, they will find moments of resonance and conflict, sometimes in places where neither seems to dwell. Do not second guess the authenticity of your emotions, for Tammi Summers has skillfully crafted a narrative that transcends the boundaries of the written word.

As we delve into *The Pond that Ripples*, let us heed her words and embrace the profound journey that awaits, where Summers invites us to witness the ripples that emanate from the depths of her soul.

—Florenza D. Lee, author of
Purpose: Life According to God's Plan

Through the ups and downs of life
And the challenges we face
We learn
We grow
But most importantly
We heal.

In space

In clouds

There is an opportunity

To see and feel

Beyond

The forces

And limitations

That anchor us to the ground.

For feet planted

Will never discover

The thrill of flight

Or

The freedom

Of

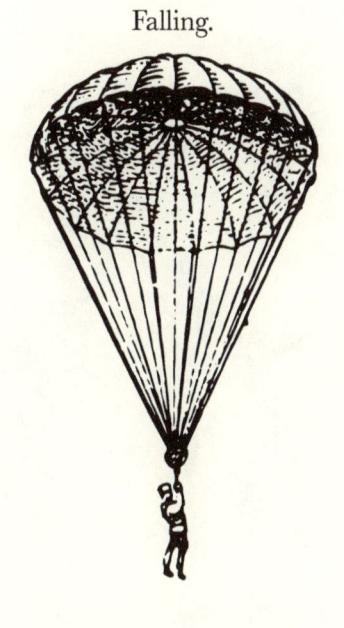

Falling.

POETRY

Justice's Pursuit

A hammer
To untempered glass
Breaks

Like the history of these United States
Written and told
Crashes
Under the weight of
Justice's Pursuit.

Shards of distortion
Descend
As the pristine
Surface
Shatters

That wall of
Rose-colored history
Falls upon its face
Its illusion of integrity
No longer
Warmly embraced.

Justice took history to trial
The verdict is clear
The judge delivered the sentence
And said,
"The time to reconcile is here."

The verdict is this:
American history
Offered a view
But did so
While
Obstructing the truth.

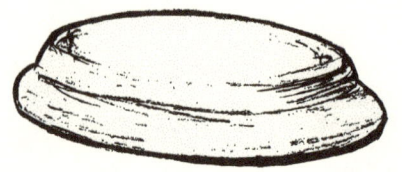

The Story of Us

I have watched our people rise from the ashes
And gather their blood into their own hands
And mold it into
The most beautiful work of art—a masterpiece.
We are permeable, malleable, flexible
Clay—we don't break!

The strength of our native land
Running through our veins
Through the roots of our hair.

Ebony and caramel skin—
Sun-soaked bodies radiant and
Beautiful—
Everlasting strength.

Our people
No one needs to define
Who we are.
One gaze
One look
Tells the Story
Of Us.

Cold Stone

A sheet of metal
A piece of rock
The ticking hands on a wall-mounted clock.
Inanimate objects groomed by pain
Lacking the depth of a human frame.

Cold as ice
Hard as stone
Minutes pass
With no audible tone.

The words from your lips
Breath's
Harmonious rise—fall—rise
The angelic gaze
Of a newborn's eyes.

These moments
Render a life worthwhile—
The tender touch of a hand
The shared warmth of a smile.

Discover Me

Look at me.
Do you see?
Beyond my exterior?
Past my physical frame?

Study me.
Inquire of my spirit
The depth of my thoughts
The story behind my name.

Find me.
Explore the hidden
Parts of my heart
The fringes
That need to be tamed.

There's beauty waiting there
In the discovery.

No Hiding

Will you endure the silence?

A soldier learns
Over the course of their days
Something's too still—
Too perfect—
Too calm—
Something's screaming
Something's wrong.

How do you hear silence?
The veteran knows
The quiet
Patience of thunder
Then ammunition
Ignites and explodes.

Rapid-fire guns
Aimed high in the night
Spread wings
As fire angels take flight.

In the blink of an eye
No safety resides
No room for escape
No places to hide.

Will you run?
Will you pray?
Will you scream?
Will you wait?

Fight as you may
To live another day
You must determine:

Will you endure the silence?

Collision

Life
In all its measurements
Of time
Experienced in segments
Seconds
Minutes
Hours
The clock's hands wind.

In a moment
That was
And is
To be
Purpose comes 'round
Full circle
When two hearts open
And finally
Speak.

Live Pursuit

Don't linger at the crossroads
Afraid to make a move.
Destiny is calling
She only waits to be pursued.

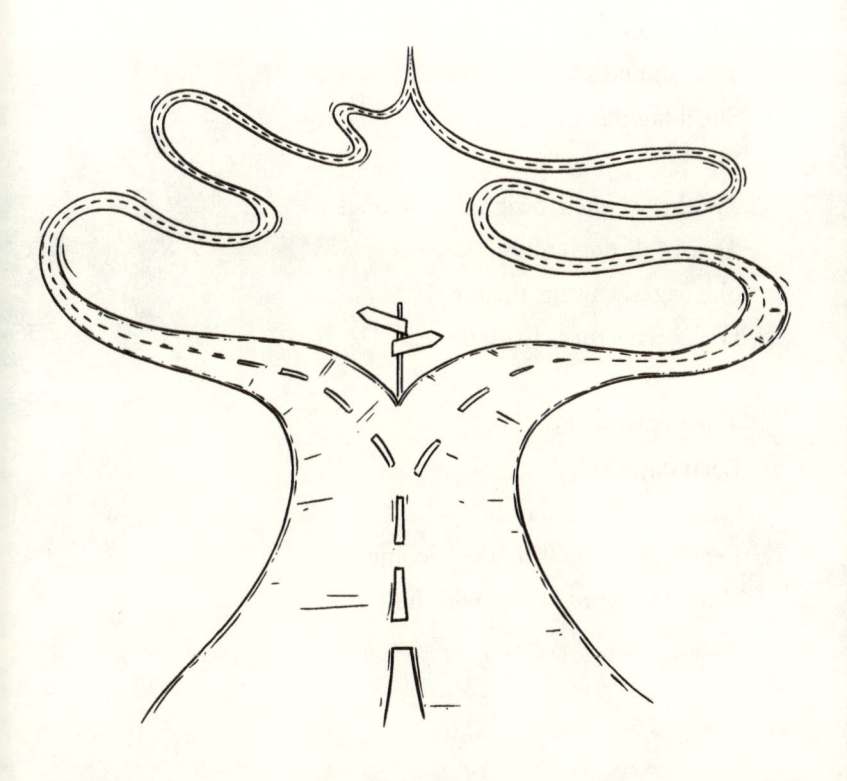

An Imperfect Woman's Prayer

Through seas of turbulence
Up the slopes of many fears
She climbs the mountains of her doubts
Above her clouds of tears.

A woman not ashamed to admit
She sometimes gets it wrong
She wants to take ownership
Her sins she must atone.

With a mustard seed of faith
She makes a solemn prayer
That should she see tomorrow
She'll handle it with care.

Another chance to right her wrongs
To love through all the sadness
She eagerly awaits the day
Her sorrow turns to gladness.

The steps she takes
Each day
One moment at a time
Lead her to who she will become:
A woman whose heart will shine.

She Dares

She's not the same woman
She used to be
She's become the woman
She dreamed she'd be.

A woman who can be anything
She dares.

A woman whose hopes become reality
For whom fear is a mere practicality
That propels her to her destiny
And beyond.

Destiny's Azimuth

Hopes and dreams
Comprise unimaginable things
Which lie sleeping, dormant,
Like peaceful, quiet streams

'Til hands and feet
Take to building,
Charting paths like magic

Setting life's course
And
Directing destiny's azimuth.

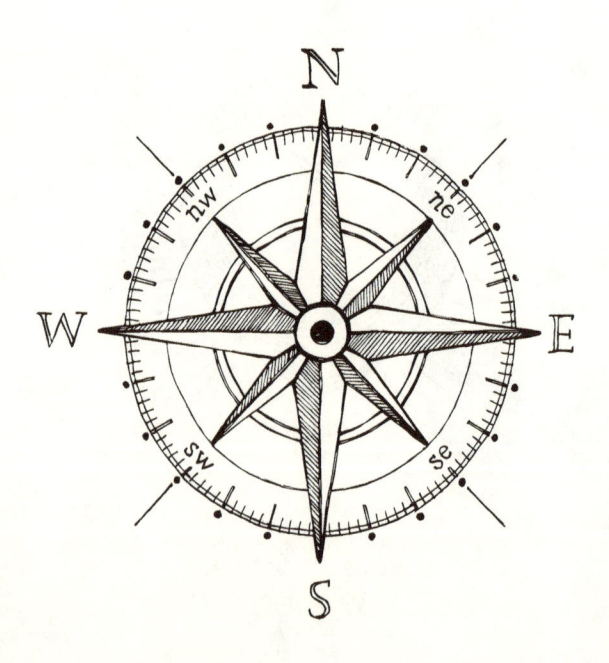

Continuum

From up above
Or down below
There are countless places
One could go.

In seas of silence
Or oceans of treasure
Time hosts realities
Of infinite measure.

Through fields of laughter
And storm-provoked tears
Canyons trace the wrinkles
Of experienced years.

In the infinite space above
Where galaxies spiral
Stars light love's path
Along life's winding highways.

Poetry

Hard to put words to feelings
It's like breaking through
A high glass ceiling.

How do you describe a heart in love
Longing for adventure?
Is it like a match
Ready to ignite its tinder?

How do you describe a love that's been lost?
Is it like the bottom of a dried-up well?
With nothing left to quench your thirst
No wind within your sail.

Or is it like the sinking of a ship
Into the depths of the sea?
The only proof of its existence
Its manifest and debris.

Hard to put words to feelings
But with rhyme
We give feeling
Meaning.

Captivate Me

In my heart, on my mind
Wishing all we had was time
Time to grow, time to know
All the places we could go.

In you
I see all of me
And the beauty that lies in between.
In a sea of endless faces
Yours
Captivates my soul.

Guiding Light

It's the light in your eyes
It's the brightness of a smile
It's the little things you do
That make life worthwhile.

We only have the moments
Which are given each day.
We never know
When the time will come
We have no more words to say.

So seize each opportunity
And don't live in fear.
Reach high enough
And your dreams will become clear.

Warm another's heart
By the kindness of your deeds.
Don't cheapen life
Through carelessness and greed.

And if your heart should ever waver
In the trials of this life
Look to heaven and His majesty
To be your guiding light.

The Father's Cocoon

Wrapped up in your warm cocoon
Protected from the world's view
Hold me close
Don't let me go
Fill me with love
'Til it overflows.

Help me mature
Inside these walls of grace.
Keep me here, Father,
In this heavenly place.

Craft my hands and mold my feet
To walk upright in my destiny.

Give my heart a new song to sing
Let your word of life lift my wings.

Companion

Upon all the roads I've traveled
Upon the mountains I've climbed
You've always been there with me
Walking by my side.

When I wake up in the morning
Or lay my head at night
You're a constant companion
And an ever-present guide.

Of all the journeys I have taken
And all the things I've been through
There is no greater joy I've found
Than being loved by you.

REFLECTIONS

Mirror, Mirror

In the looking glass,
You will not find
The divine encounter you seek,
For what you see will certainly fade away.

Shine Bright

In the light there are no shadows.
No darkness appears.
Only rays of hope for tomorrow
And purposes made clear.

Human

The weight of perfection
Will drag down
Even the lightest of souls.

It is only when we accept
Our imperfection
That we free ourselves from pride

And then extend grace
Not only to ourselves,
But to all humanity.

Flesh and Blood

We try to hold on
So tightly
To this world—
To make a name for ourselves
So we're not forgotten
Once we're gone.

We must realize
The only things
That last forever
Are the impressions
We make
In flesh and blood
In hearts and souls
Everything else will fade.

Ears to Hear

You can tell a story a thousand times
But it's like the first time
When it falls on the right ears.

Love Freely

The essence of true love
Is to love
Freely
With no expectations
No fear

Wide open
To experience
The beauty that exists
In that moment
With that person
Whom you love.

The Hard Parts

I've grown accustomed
To saying goodbye
But I like it less and less
Each time.

Letting go
On the other hand
Is a skill I must master
And must do so gracefully.

Survive

You survive depression.
Every day is a battle within your mind.
Some days are easier than others.
You must choose to defend your life –
To remind yourself that your life is worth defending.
You are not alone.
You're worth every bit of energy it takes
 To stare depression down
And say,
"You will not win!"

Synchronize

We often let imaginary boundaries and barriers
Physically stop us from pursuing our purpose.
When we realize there is nothing
That prevents us from achieving
What we've set our minds to do
The next step
Is to train our brains and feet
To move in concert.

Thoughts

Thoughts are powerful and potentially dangerous.
Thoughts are the beginning of innovation and, for some,
The trail that leads to demise.
But harness your thoughts and wield them for good
And no negativity will dissuade you from your resolve
To think positively about yourself
To embrace the impact you can make on others
And the opportunities that lie before you.

Perspective

Many people decide to thrive.
Some unfortunately fold.
The good thing about perspective, though,
Is the opportunity
To re-read the story that's been told.

Precepts

Letting go of perfection—Freedom

Striving for excellence—Passion

Never giving up—Resilience

Forgiving yourself and others—Peace

Looking beyond your line of sight—Vision

Seeing it all happen before it does—Faith

Her

If you find a woman
Who has discovered
Her voice, value, and vision
Then you have found a woman
 Who is ready
To face the world and conquer it.

Sometimes silence speaks louder—
Less is more—
And sometimes
Greatness takes time.

Scars

Some cover them.
Some have them removed.
Some camouflage them with a smile.

However you choose to deal with them
The fact remains that we all carry them.

So remember
When you meet someone:
They, like you, have scar tissue.

Help to heal their pain
By covering them
With love and kindness.

Regeneration

Life isn't always sunshine and roses.

Sometimes we get pricked by thorns.

Other times, we are burned.

But there is life after pain

And there is beauty that rises from the ashes.

Love's Light

Love, realized and actualized,
Is like a light
That shines in the darkness
And illuminates
The very depths of the human soul.

Love can't be seen—
Yet it can reach you,
If you let it.

Beyond the Sun

Above the fog
Clouds float high.
Through the clouds
The sun, moon, and stars
Light up the sky.
Beyond the stars lies eternity.

QUOTES

There was you
and me
and everything in between.

You'll be surprised what you find
when you stop romancing
and start communicating.

Have enough love to share
that you don't need a return on the investment.
Love spent is love worth spending.

When peace lives within your heart
there is no need to go and find it.

Something I find
more attractive than confidence
is generosity—

a genuine love for people
demonstrated by actions.

There is nothing more beautiful
than a heart set in motion.

The preponderance of time
reveals that
in time,
all things are revealed.

Many will appreciate your beauty,
but not many will value your heart.
Wait for the one who honors your spirit
and protects your reputation.

You don't need anyone's permission
to take charge
of your life.

Sometimes we're forced in directions
we ought
to have found for ourselves.

Humans
are often anxious to improve their circumstances
but unwilling to improve themselves.
They therefore remain bound.

The past was never intended to be
a permanent dwelling.

Don't look back on the past.
Rearview mirrors are for driving.

Don't let tomorrow rob you
of all that today
has to offer.

I've wanted to be everything
and, at the same time,
nothing at all.

To see another's heart,
you must look past
your own.

She discovered peace
in the place where she found truth.

When all's said and done,
you really are
who you are
on the inside.

The heart is what creates vibrancy,
renders authenticity,
and lends credibility
to the
human experience.

To be in a position
to forget your position
and
remember your humanity—that is the beginning
of compassionate leadership.

Remember, the value of your productivity relies on the value you place in the people producing for you.

When considering what it takes to be a
compassionate leader,
remember to remain
H.U.M.B.L.E.

H—Help others, Heed wisdom
U—Undergo change, Uplift others
M—Motivate, Move forward with a positive attitude
B—Be yourself, Be caring, Be confident
L—Lead with love in mind: Love people, Love your country, Love God
E—Exemplify excellence, energetically, daily

Success is great for morale—but challenges build character.

Tammi Lynn Summers is a native of Columbus, Georgia. Growing up as a military child, she moved with her father, mother, and siblings from country to country and state to state. Seeing the world at an early age opened Tammi's eyes and enabled her to gain an appreciation for diverse cultures and their history.

Tammi received her bachelor's degree in communications from Columbus State University and received her master's degree in cybersecurity at Norfolk State University. In May 2007, Tammi became a commissioned officer in the United States Army. As an officer, Tammi has lived in various places, completed three combat tours to Afghanistan, and one operational assignment to Kuwait.

Tammi's mantra is to pursue God passionately. Through this mantra Tammi wrote, recorded, and produced her first music album, *In the Making*, with popular songs titled "Keep it in the Middle" and "Walk by Faith," which may be found on SoundCloud. Tammi also co-wrote, with her twin sister Tifani, the lyrics for Columbus, Georgia's Northside High School anthem, titled, "O' Northside High, O' Northside High." In 2019, Tammi's original song "Cancer Found Me" was selected to be performed at the annual American Cancer Society's peninsula breast cancer walk.

Tammi's poem "Moving Forward" won the 2016 Fort Hood Black History Month Poetry Contest. In the same year, "Moving Forward" was also published in volume three of Texas A&M's literary journal, *The Lookout*.

When off duty, Tammi can be found volunteering in her community, attending seminars and forums, and supporting her local church. As a Christian, her greatest desire in life and in service is to please God while loving people.

www.ingramcontent.com/pod-product-compliance
Lightning Source LLC
LaVergne TN
LVHW091248201224
799494LV00010B/337